COOKING THE
THE
CENTRAL AMERICAN
WAY

Lerner Publications Company
A division of Lerner Publishing Group
241 First Avenue North
Minneapolis, MN 55401 U.S.A.

Website address: www.lernerbooks.com

Library of Congress Cataloging-in-Publication Data

Behnke, Alison.
    Cooking the Central American way / by Alison M. Behnke, Griselda Aracely Chacon, and Kristina Anderson.
       p.   cm. — (Easy menu ethnic cookbooks)
    Includes index.
    ISBN: 0–8225–1236–X (lib. bdg. : alk. paper)
     1. Cookery—Central America—Juvenile literature. I. Chacon, Griselda Aracely. II. Anderson, Kristina. III. Title. IV. Series.
    TX716.A1B445 2005
    641.59728—dc22   2004011870

Manufactured in the United States of America
1 2 3 4 5 6 – JR – 10 09 08 07 06 05

easy menu ethnic cookbooks

COOKING

culturally authentic foods

THE

including low-fat and

CENTRAL AMERICAN

vegetarian recipes

WAY

Alison Behnke in consultation with Griselda Aracely Chacon and Kristina Anderson

Lerner Publications Company • Minneapolis

Contents

Introduction

Central America is a slender bridge of land stretching between North and South America, with the Pacific Ocean to the west and the Caribbean Sea to the east. Scattered across this bridge, called an isthmus, are the seven small countries of Belize, Guatemala, El Salvador, Honduras, Nicaragua, Costa Rica, and Panama. These nations share many connections in their climates, histories, cultures, and—most deliciously—in their culinary customs.

Modern Central America showcases a rich blend of influences, drawing from ancient civilizations and a more recent era of European colonization. The region bridges the divide between North and South America with a flavorful cuisine that mixes the best of both continents. Central America offers cooks and diners alike a tempting range of sweet and spicy selections that keep everyone coming back for more.

These stuffed tortillas may be filled with pork, cheese, or beans. (Recipe on pages 40-41.)

BELIZE
★Belmopan

GUATEMALA
Guatemala
City ★

HONDURAS

San ★
Salvador

★Tegucigalpa

EL SALVADOR

NICARAGUA

★Managua

Caribbean Sea

PACIFIC
OCEAN

San José★

COSTA
RICA

PANAMA
City
★

PANAMA

The Land and Its History

Lying squarely in the tropics, Central America has hot, humid weather year-round. This climate has given the region a wealth of rain forests, especially on the eastern side of the isthmus. These jungles are home to some of the world's rarest and most precious plants and animals, as well as stunning Mayan ruins. Although much of the forest is endangered due to harvesting and clearing for farms, homes, and roads, many environmental groups are working to save it.

Central America is mostly mountainous, with the large Sierra Madre range dominating the landscapes of Guatemala, El Salvador, and Honduras. Farther south, smaller ranges, including the Cordillera de Talamanca and the Serrania de Tabasara, rise in Costa Rica and Panama. On the western coast of Central America, these picturesque mountains blanketed in lush greenery are part of the dangerous Anillo de Fuego (Ring of Fire) that circles the Pacific Ocean. The region is dotted with active volcanoes, and earthquakes strike frequently.

Within Central America's mountains and jungles lie the ruins of the great Mayan Empire, established close to three thousand years ago. This remarkable civilization enjoyed its greatest glory between about A.D. 250 and 900. Mayan leaders, scientists, priests, and artists developed advanced systems of government, religion, and society. Although the culture mysteriously crumbled in about 900, its legacy lives on in the form of magnificent pyramids, ancient writings, and the customs and stories passed down among the modern Maya.

After the Mayan Empire declined, a new empire sent its forces to the region. In the late 1400s and early 1500s, conquistadors (conquerors) arrived from Spain, exploring and colonizing the Americas.

These Mayan ruins at Tikal, Guatemala, were built beginning around 600 B.C.

Vasco de Balboa, a famous conquistador, crossed Panama on foot in 1513. He was the first European to see the Pacific Ocean.

The Caribbean islands, South America, and Mexico were conquered first. Hungry for still greater treasures of gold, silver, and other precious goods, the conquistadors soon turned their attention to Central America. Descendants of the Maya and other native peoples resisted conquest by the advancing Spaniards. However, local populations were often divided into many separate subgroups, and these individual forces could not match the Spanish in numbers or weaponry. Further weakened by new diseases brought from Europe, thousands of Maya and other native peoples were killed as Spain's armies swept across the isthmus.

Throughout Central America, Spanish colonists forced the native people into backbreaking labor on large farms called plantations. Growing valuable crops such as cotton and cacao (used for making chocolate), these farms yielded great wealth for the Spanish settlers. Meanwhile, the local population grew poorer and weaker.

In the 1700s, growing demand for labor on the plantations led to the beginning of the trans-Atlantic slave trade in the Americas. Thousands of Africans were forced onto crowded ships and brought across the ocean, facing hardship and misery in their new homes. Although relatively few slaves came to Central America compared to its neighbors of North and South America, some slaves did arrive there. They mingled with the local population, as did immigrants from the Caribbean islands to the northeast, bringing new cultural and culinary influences to the region.

By the early 1800s, most residents of the Central American colonies had grown tired of Spanish rule. Independence movements began to ripple through the region, toppling colonial governments. Independence did not bring calm, however, as conflicts arose among and within the young nations. In addition, the introduction of coffee crops in the late 1800s created new wealth but also new strife by widening the gap between rich and poor.

Over the course of the 1900s, many of Central America's nations struggled with issues including civil war and harsh governments. Nevertheless, these countries also have many resources to draw upon. In the early 2000s, the region's people take great pride in the area's cultural diversity and its great strength in the face of hardship.

The Food

Central America's history of intermingling cultures led to the exchange of different foods and cooking techniques. Spanish conquistadors had found unfamiliar crops such as corn, tomatoes, hot peppers, and squash in the Americas. Regional cooks had long used these ingredients as the basis of their cuisine. With the arrival of the colonists, important new crops such as wheat joined the native foods. The Spanish introduced chickens, pigs, and cattle to the region, adding more meat, eggs, and milk to Central American diets. Residents combined these ingredients with local fruits and vegetables to create new kinds of dishes. The Spanish also brought a taste for sweets. When they were introduced to the Central American flavors of vanilla and chocolate, they used them in combination with their own crop of sugarcane to create delicious dessert recipes.

Ripe, red coffee beans are harvested by a worker in Costa Rica.

Modern Central American farmers—aided by the region's fertile volcanic soil—still cultivate ancient crops and newer Spanish additions, producing a wealth of different foods. In Belize farmers raise sugarcane, along with delicious tropical fruits such as bananas and papayas. In neighboring Guatemala, important crops include corn, the spice cardamom, and valuable coffee beans. El Salvador, too, is home to crops of coffee, sugarcane, and corn, along with beans and rice, and Hondurans harvest pineapples, melons, and citrus fruits. Farther south, Nicaraguan farmers raise peanuts, coffee, bananas, sesame, and soybeans, while Costa Ricans farm foods such as plantains (a relative of the banana), rice, beans, and potatoes. Panamanians produce harvests of coffee, bananas, sugarcane, and vegetables.

Fishing crews throughout Central America also pull in valuable catches of fish, shrimp, and other seafood along the coasts. Farther inland, farmers tend to livestock such as cattle and sheep, and in rural areas, many households keep a few pigs and chickens of their own in yards or nearby fields.

Luckily for local diners, this wide range of resources has given Central America a diverse culinary tradition. Regional cooks are masters at using the best produce and grains to create fresh, delicious meals. The blending of native tastes with the Spanish colonists' favorite foods also brought new variety to Central American tables, as did influences from African slaves and Caribbean immigrants.

Many popular dishes are eaten by diners throughout the region, crossing borders and connecting people of different nations, ethnic groups, and lifestyles. One of these common foods is *sopa de frijoles* (bean soup). While variations exist from country to country and cook to cook, this simple, hearty soup is found all around Central America. Other widespread favorites are fried plantains, countless variations on basic rice and beans, and rich desserts such as *arroz con leche* (rice pudding).

A host of national specialties also exists. Guatemalan cooks take great pride in their *pepian*, a thick stew of chicken and potatoes in a rich tomato, pepper, and pumpkin seed sauce. Guatemalans also enjoy *escabeche*, a tart salad of pickled vegetables, and jocon—meat in a green sauce of cilantro, green onions, and tomatillos (a relative of the tomato).

In the nations of Belize and Honduras, which lie in northern Central America, nearby Caribbean islands have lent their flavors to local cuisine. Favorites here include tropical-tasting *pan de coco* (coconut bread), along with Caribbean standards such as johnny cakes (biscuits) and fried fish. Other Belizean favorites are stewed chicken and stewed beans, prepared by slowly cooking the chicken, beans, or other main ingredients in a thick, spicy sauce. Honduran diners feast on specialties such as *sopa de caracol*, a thick soup made with conch (a type of shellfish), coconut milk, and potatoes or yucca (a root vegetable similar in texture to a potato). Another popular dish in Honduras is *pinchos*, grilled meat kabobs often served with vegetables, beans, and cheese.

In El Salvador, nearly everyone eats *pupusas*, cornmeal cakes stuffed with cheese, beans, or meat and served with salsa and a zesty vegetable slaw. After an especially spicy plate of pupusas, Salvadorans cool down with sweet rice milk called *horchata*. A favorite dessert is Maria Luisa cake, a fresh-tasting layer cake flavored with orange juice, orange zest, and orange marmalade.

Nicaraguans have a sweet tooth too, and the famous *tres leches* cake is a traditional treat here, as well as in Costa Rica and other Central American nations. Tres leches translates to "three milks," and the cake is soaked with evaporated milk, sweetened condensed milk, and cream or whole milk. Nicaraguan entrées tend to have a lot of meat, such as *indio viejo*, a porridgelike dish of beef, cornmeal, vegetables, and mint. Nicaraguan *churrasco* is grilled meat—usually beef—served with a zesty onion and parsley sauce, and another national classic is *vigoron*, boiled yucca topped with fried pork. Both Nicaraguans and Costa Ricans claim a rice and bean dish called *gallo pinto* as a national specialty, and Costa Ricans also enjoy *enyucados*, fried yucca fritters flavored with cilantro.

In Panama, a narrow country with many miles of coastline, seafood figures highly in dishes such as *seviche*. This cold seafood salad is made with shrimp or raw fish, vegetables, citrus juice, and spices. Plantains are also a Panamanian favorite, and they are served fried, baked, mashed, as a salty snack, and even as a sweet dessert.

Holidays and Festivals

Before Europeans arrived in Central America, ancient Mayan religion guided many areas of the local people's lives. Festivals, ceremonies, and rituals honoring their many gods and goddesses were held almost daily. When the Spanish arrived in the Americas, they brought with them their own religion: Catholicism, a branch of Christianity. To convert the local people to Catholicism, the colonists forbade traditional religions and destroyed many Mayan temples and documents. However, some Maya secretly continued to observe many of their long-held beliefs and traditions. These practices eventually blended with Christianity to create a new and unique belief system, which is followed by many of the region's people. Smaller populations of Jews and Muslims also live in Central America.

Largely as a result of this rich religious past, Central Americans celebrate a great many holidays and festivals. In the Christian tradition, Easter and Christmas are the year's two most important events. All throughout the region, Semana Santa—the week leading up to Easter—is a time for dramatic and emotional festivities. Small villages and large cities alike hold processions in which worshippers carry statues of Jesus, Mary, and other Christian figures through the streets to or from the local church.

One of the most beautiful Easter traditions in the region takes place in the city of Antigua, Guatemala. The night before Good Friday (the Friday before Easter), residents spend many hours creating intricate, brightly colored carpets of flower petals and dyed sawdust in the sidewalks and streets. Then, beginning at dawn on Good Friday, large processions pass over these temporary works of art, destroying the display until the next year. On Easter Sunday, many Central Americans attend a morning Mass (Catholic church

Guatemalans celebrate Semana Santa with an elaborate procession.

service). Afterward, they head home to enjoy large feasts with family and friends. This celebration meal showcases many regional specialties, along with holiday treats. Many Catholics do not eat meat or fish during the forty days before Easter, called Lent, so meat and seafood figure prominently on holiday menus. For dessert, people all around the area snack on sweet *polvorones*, buttery cookies rolled in powdered sugar. In Costa Rica, traditional Easter foods are rice pudding and *dulce de chiverre* (sweet fruit preserves).

Children in Central America especially love the Christmas holiday. In many countries, children take part in *las posadas*, which last from December 16 until Christmas Eve. In this cherished tradition, families and neighbors walk through the town visiting homes and acting out the Christmas story, sometimes donning costumes and carrying candles. Young Salvadorans also play a special role in their holiday celebrations, singing holiday songs at church and in people's homes. In addition to carols, traditional native music is very popular at Christmastime. Many homes are decorated with nativity scenes depicting the Christmas story, along with lights, wreaths, and tropical flowers. Costa Ricans put up Christmas trees that may be small cypress trees or made from dried evergreen or coffee branches.

Celebrations peak on Christmas Eve. In Honduras and Belize, communities of Garífuna (descendants of African slaves and indigenous Caribbean people) take to the streets as women perform traditional dances to the accompaniment of drums played by the men. These festivities often last all night and into Christmas. Many Central Americans light fireworks at midnight, making for a noisy walk to the Misa de Gallo (Rooster's Mass), which begins at midnight and ends very early on Christmas morning—sometimes around the time the roosters begin crowing! Some people like to eat the holiday dinner before the church service, while others eat when they return home. Either way, the feast is always a special one.

In all Central American countries, *tamales* are a classic Christmas specialty. These packets of cornmeal batter are stuffed with meat or bean fillings, cooked in cornhusks or banana leaves, and opened like delicious holiday gifts. Chicken soup is also a favorite dish all around the region, and many cooks prepare recipes that date back to Mayan times. Honduran cooks make special rice dishes with shrimp, vegetables, and spices, while Nicaraguans and Panamanians eat similar rice dishes made with chicken and flavored with the herb saffron. Desserts, such as the Salvadoran *pan de torta* (a sweet, dense holiday bread) and Panamanian fruitcake, are also popular. Hondurans and other Central Americans like to drink sweet, thick eggnog, as well. Christmas Day itself is relatively quiet, and many people visit friends and family to wish each other holiday greetings and to exchange gifts.

Central Americans observe other holidays throughout the year. Some of these are secular (nonreligious), such as the various nations' Independence Day celebrations, while the *fiestas patronales* are the feast days of individual Catholic saints. One popular event that blends Mayan and Christian ideas is the combined holiday of All Saints' Day and All Souls' Day (also known as Day of the Dead). Honoring deceased ancestors, the holiday is both a Christian feast day and a celebration with roots in the ancient Mayan festival Hanal Pixan. In Guatemala people fly kites in local cemeteries and prepare *fiambre*, a dish of cooked meats and marinated vegetables. Around the region, a number of other popular holiday treats, such as tamales and baked pumpkin, are prepared in a special way. The traditional practice of burying the foods in a fire pit and then removing them symbolizes death and the rising of the soul to an afterlife.

The many holidays and festivals of Central America make it truly a region of celebrations. And much to the delight of hungry festivalgoers, there are always plenty of delicious treats to make each occasion even more special.

Before You Begin

Central American cooking makes use of some ingredients that you may not know. Sometimes special cookware is used too, although the recipes in this book can easily be prepared with ordinary utensils and pans.

The most important thing you need to know before you start is how to be a careful cook. On the following page, you'll find a few rules that will make your cooking experience safe, fun, and easy. Next, take a look at the "dictionary" of utensils, terms, and special ingredients. You may also want to read the list of tips on preparing healthy, low-fat meals.

When you've picked out a recipe to try, read through it from beginning to end. Then you are ready to shop for ingredients and to organize the cookware you will need. Once you have assembled everything, you're ready to begin cooking.

Johnny cakes, a type of biscuit from Belize, make a great addition to any meal. Here they are served with fried fish. (Recipes on pages 33 and 51.)

The Careful Cook

Whenever you cook, there are certain safety rules you must always keep in mind. Even experienced cooks follow these rules when they are in the kitchen.

- Always wash your hands before handling food. Thoroughly wash all raw vegetables and fruits to remove dirt, chemicals, and insecticides. Wash uncooked poultry, fish, and meat under cold water.
- Use a cutting board when cutting up vegetables and fruits. Don't cut them up in your hand! And be sure to cut in a direction *away* from you and your fingers.
- Long hair or loose clothing can easily catch fire if brought near the burners of a stove. If you have long hair, tie it back before you start cooking.
- Turn all pot handles toward the back of the stove so that you will not catch your sleeves or jewelry on them. This is especially important when younger brothers and sisters are around. They could easily knock off a pot and get burned.
- Always use a pot holder to steady hot pots or to take pans out of the oven. Don't use a wet cloth on a hot pan because the steam it produces could burn you.
- Lift the lid of a steaming pot with the opening away from you so you will not get burned.
- If you get burned, hold the burn under cold running water. Do not put grease or butter on it. Cold water helps to take the heat out, but grease or butter will only keep it in.
- If grease or cooking oil catches fire, throw baking soda or salt at the bottom of the flame to put it out. (Water will *not* put out a grease fire.) Call for help, and try to turn all the stove burners to "off."

Cooking Utensils

cheesecloth—A gauzy cotton cloth that can be used to strain food. It is sold in most grocery stores.

colander—A bowl-shaped dish with holes in it that is used for washing or draining food

grater—A utensil with sharp-edged holes, used to grade or shred food into small pieces

ladle—A deep-bowled, long-handled spoon used for serving soups and other liquids. To ladle something means to serve with a ladle.

sieve—A bowl-shaped utensil made of wire mesh, used to drain food

spatula—A flat, thin utensil used to lift, toss, turn, or scoop up food

whisk—A wire utensil used for beating food by hand

wire rack—An open wire stand on which hot food is cooled

Cooking Terms

beat—To stir rapidly in a circular motion

broil—To cook directly under a heat source so that the side of the food facing the heat cooks rapidly

brown—To cook food quickly over high heat so that the surface turns an even brown

chop—To cut into small pieces

cube—To cut into small, cube-shaped pieces

garnish—To decorate with small pieces of food such as sprigs of fresh herbs

knead—To work dough by pressing it with the palms, pushing it outward, and then pressing it over on itself

preheat—To allow an oven to warm up to a certain temperature before putting food in it puree—To press food through a food mill or to process it in a blender or food processor until it is a smooth, thick pulp called a puree

sauté—To fry quickly over high heat in oil or butter, stirring or turning the food to prevent burning

seed—To remove seeds from a food

sift—To mix several dry ingredients together or to remove lumps in dry ingredients by putting them through a sieve or sifter

simmer—To cook over low heat in liquid kept just below its boiling point. Bubbles may occasionally rise to the surface.

Special Ingredients

achiote paste—Also called annatto paste, a seasoning made from the seeds of the annatto tree, along with spices and salt. It is used to add golden color to food.

basil—A rich, fragrant herb whose fresh or dried leaves are used in cooking

bay leaves—The dried leaves of the bay (also called laurel) tree

capers—Flower buds of the caper bush, pickled and sold in jars

chile peppers—Hot peppers. Chiles used in Central American cooking include the very hot guajillo, pasilla, jalapeño, and Mexican chili (chile guaque). If you do not eat spicy food very often, try a milder pepper such as poblano, Anaheim, or pimiento before moving on to hotter chiles.

chives—A member of the onion family whose thin, green stalks are chopped and usually used fresh

cider vinegar—Vinegar made from apple cider, with a slightly fruity flavor

cilantro—An herb used fresh as a flavoring and garnish. Dried, ground cilantro is known as coriander.

cinnamon—A spice made from the bark of a tree in the laurel family. Cinnamon is available ground or in sticks.

coconut milk—A rich liquid made by simmering shredded coconut meat with water. Look for coconut milk or reduced-fat (light) coconut milk in your grocery or health food store, or at Latin American or Asian markets.

corn oil—A cooking oil made from corn kernels

crushed red pepper flakes—Dried flakes and seeds of hot red peppers

masa harina—Finely ground cornmeal processed with a chemical called lime and used to make tortillas

oregano—A pungent herb in the mint family, used fresh or dried—and either whole or ground—as a seasoning

plantain—A starchy fruit that resembles a banana but must be peeled and cooked before it is eaten

pumpkin seeds—Dried, edible seeds of squash or pumpkin. Also called *pepitas*, pumpkin seeds for Central American recipes can be found at most Latin American and Mexican markets.

red wine vinegar—Vinegar made from red wine, with a deep, rich flavor

saffron—A spice from the crocus flower that has a strong flavor and adds a yellow color to foods. Saffron is available in threads or in a powdered form. Powdered saffron is less expensive and easier to use than saffron threads. If saffron is too expensive, Central American cooks often use the spice turmeric instead. Although the flavor will be different, turmeric gives dishes the same bright yellow color that saffron does.

tomatillo—A small green fruit that is related to the tomato, with a papery outer husk that must be removed before using. Tomatillos are popular in Central American cooking and can be found at supermarkets and at most Latin American and Mexican markets.

vanilla extract—A liquid made from vanilla beans and used to flavor foods, especially desserts

yucca—A root vegetable, similar in texture to a potato. Also called cassava, yucca can be baked, mashed, or fried.

Healthy and Low-Fat Cooking Tips

Many modern cooks are concerned about preparing healthy, low-fat meals. Fortunately, there are simple ways to reduce the fat content of most dishes. Here are a few general tips for adapting the recipes in this book. Throughout the book, you'll also find specific suggestions for individual recipes—and don't worry, they'll still taste delicious!

Many recipes call for oil to sauté vegetables or other ingredients. If you like, you can reduce the amount of oil you use. You can also substitute a low-fat or nonfat cooking spray for oil. Sprinkling a little salt on the vegetables brings out their natural juices, so less oil is needed. It's also a good idea to use a small, nonstick frying pan if you decide to use less oil than the recipe calls for. When recipes call for deep-frying in oil, you may want to experiment with baking the dish to reduce fat.

Central American cooking traditionally uses a lot of meat. Buying extra-lean meats and trimming off as much fat as possible are two simple ways to keep your meal healthy. If you are a vegetarian or if you just want to reduce the fat content of your meal, cutting meat out of a dish is a simple solution. In some dishes, you can replace meat with a substantial vegetable such as potatoes. Or, if you want to keep a source of protein in your dish, there are many low-fat options. Try using a vegetarian alternative to meat, such as tofu, tempeh, or mock duck. However, using these ingredients will change the flavor of a dish, so you may need to experiment a little bit to decide if you like these substitutions.

There are many ways to prepare authentic meals that are good for you and still taste great. As you become a more experienced cook, try experimenting with recipes and substitutions to find the methods that work best for you.

METRIC CONVERSIONS

Cooks in the United States measure both liquid and solid ingredients using standard containers based on the 8-ounce cup and the tablespoon. These measurements are based on volume, while the metric system of measurement is based on both weight (for solids) and volume (for liquids). To convert from U.S. fluid tablespoons, ounces, quarts, and so forth to metric liters is a straightforward conversion, using the chart below. However, since solids have different weights—one cup of rice does not weigh the same as one cup of grated cheese, for example—many cooks who use the metric system have kitchen scales to weigh different ingredients. The chart below will give you a good starting point for basic conversions to the metric system.

MASS (weight)

1 ounce (oz.)	=	28.0 grams (g)
8 ounces	=	227.0 grams
1 pound (lb.) or 16 ounces	=	0.45 kilograms (kg)
2.2 pounds	=	1.0 kilogram

LIQUID VOLUME

1 teaspoon (tsp.)	=	5.0 milliliters (ml)
1 tablespoon (tbsp.)	=	15.0 milliliters
1 fluid ounce (oz.)	=	30.0 milliliters
1 cup (c.)	=	240 milliliters
1 pint (pt.)	=	480 milliliters
1 quart (qt.)	=	0.95 liters (l)
1 gallon (gal.)	=	3.80 liters

LENGTH

¼ inch (in.)	=	0.6 centimeters (cm)
½ inch	=	1.25 centimeters
1 inch	=	2.5 centimeters

TEMPERATURE

212°F	=	100°C (boiling point of water)
225°F	=	110°C
250°F	=	120°C
275°F	=	135°C
300°F	=	150°C
325°F	=	160°C
350°F	=	180°C
375°F	=	190°C
400°F	=	200°C

(To convert temperature in Fahrenheit to Celsius, subtract 32 and multiply by .56)

PAN SIZES

8-inch cake pan	= 20 x 4-centimeter cake pan
9-inch cake pan	= 23 x 3.5-centimeter cake pan
11 x 7-inch baking pan	= 28 x 18-centimeter baking pan
13 x 9-inch baking pan	= 32.5 x 23-centimeter baking pan
9 x 5-inch loaf pan	= 23 x 13-centimeter loaf pan
2-quart casserole	= 2-liter casserole

A Central American Table

Many Central American homes are quite modest. Sometimes several generations of a family live together in a small house or apartment, and rural areas and small villages often lack modern conveniences. As a result, Central American tables are often quite crowded and very simply set. But to most people in the region, the really important thing about the table is who gathers around it. Daily meals—especially lunch, which is the largest meal of the day for most people—give families a chance to relax and chat about the day's events. Breakfast and dinner are typically lighter than the midday meal, with breakfast often little more than coffee and a piece of toast. Dinner is also a small meal, usually consisting of only one or two dishes.

Guatemalans gather in front of a church to share a meal.

A Central American Menu

Below are suggested menus for a large Central American lunch, along with a lighter supper. Also included are shopping lists of the ingredients you'll need to prepare these meals. These are just a few possible combinations of dishes and flavors. As you gain more experience with Central American cooking, you may enjoy planning your own menus.

LUNCH

Fried plantains

Bean soup

Grilled beef with parsley sauce

Powdered sugar cookies

SHOPPING LIST:

Produce

2 ripe (yellow-and-black skinned) plantains
1 red or green bell pepper
1 small yellow onion
1 small white onion
1 head garlic
1 bunch green onions
1 bunch fresh cilantro
1 bunch fresh parsley

Dairy/Egg/Meat

1 c. (2 sticks) butter or margarine
4 to 6 large eggs (optional)
1 lb. beef tenderloin

Canned/Bottled/Boxed

3 15-oz. cans black or red beans

Miscellaneous

red wine vinegar
corn oil
olive or vegetable oil
flour
powdered sugar
vanilla extract
salt
black pepper

SUPPER

Johnny cakes

Fried fish

Rice milk

SHOPPING LIST:

Produce

4 limes

Dairy/Egg/Meat

¼ c. (½ stick) butter or
    vegetable shortening

4 to 6 whitefish fillets (about
    1 lb.)
2 large eggs
6 tbsp. milk

Canned/Bottled/Boxed

12 oz. coconut milk

Miscellaneous

corn or vegetable oil
flour
unseasoned bread crumbs
    (optional)
rice
sugar
baking powder
vanilla extract
cinnamon sticks or ground
    cinnamon
salt
black pepper

Starters and Side Dishes

The great variety of Central American cooking really stands out in the cuisine's wide selection of appetizers and side dishes. Ranging from light to substantial, simple to fancy, there's something for everyone.

For example, delicate Panamanian seviche is the perfect hors d'oeuvre for a dressy dinner or party, while filling coconut bread is a fitting side for an everyday family meal. These starters and sides also offer plenty of choices to vegetarians and meat eaters alike. While crispy *carimañolas* (yucca fritters) can be filled with ground beef, they're just as delicious with rice, veggies, or tofu. Likewise, Salvadoran pupusas are most commonly made with a cheese stuffing, but meat lovers can substitute beef, pork, or chicken for a heavier dish. Johnny cakes—biscuits that may once have been called "journey cakes" and carried by travelers in the Caribbean— are a perfect snack for people on the go. Crispy fried plantains can satisfy a craving for either salty or sweet flavors. All in all, with so many delicious choices, a Central American side dish can easily steal the show!

In El Salvador, stuffed tortillas are served with plenty of hot sauce. (Recipe on page 40.)

Coconut Bread/Pan de Coco (Belize, Honduras)

Along the Caribbean coasts of Central American nations such as Belize and Honduras, coconut bread is a staple similar to corn tortillas in other parts of the region. Pan de coco is served with nearly every meal in these coastal areas.

3 c. flour

2 tsp. baking soda

½ tsp. salt

1 c. coconut milk*

1 tsp. vanilla extract

vegetable or corn oil for preparing pan

*For bread with an extra coconut kick, add 2 to 4 tbsp. grated unsweetened coconut to the mixture in Step 2 and sprinkle some coconut over the top of the loaf before baking.

1. Preheat oven to 325°F.

2. In a large mixing bowl, combine flour, baking soda, and salt. Mix well.

3. In a smaller bowl, combine coconut milk and vanilla. Add to flour mixture and mix well.

4. Remove dough from bowl. On a clean countertop or other work surface, knead dough until smooth and elastic. If dough seems too hard, add 1 tsp. at a time of extra coconut milk or water as necessary. If it is too runny, add 1 tsp. of flour at a time.

5. Press dough into a lightly oiled loaf pan, smoothing out any large lumps that remain. Use a fork to poke a few holes in the top of the loaf.

6. Bake 45 to 55 minutes, or until golden brown. Remove from oven and cool in pan for 10 minutes. Turn out onto wire rack and let cool completely. Coconut bread is best if eaten within a day or two of baking.

Preparation time: 20 minutes
Baking time: 45 to 55 minutes
Makes 1 loaf

Johnny Cakes (Belize)

Not to be confused with North American johnny cakes, which may be cornmeal pancakes or cornbread, these Belizean specialties are more like biscuits. And while they are often served with breakfast, topped with butter or salty cheese, they are also popular at other times of the day, with any meal.

2½ c. flour plus extra for kneading

4 tsp. baking powder

¼ tsp. salt

¼ c. (½ stick) butter or vegetable shortening, room temperature

1½ c. coconut milk

1. In a large bowl, combine flour, baking powder, and salt. Mix well.

2. Using your hands, rub butter or shortening into flour mixture until it becomes grainy. With a spoon, slowly stir in coconut milk until dough can be formed into a ball and is not too sticky to work with.

3. On a clean, lightly floured countertop or other work surface, knead dough for about 10 minutes. Shape dough into balls about 2 inches in diameter and place on an ungreased baking sheet. Place balls about 1 inch apart and flatten slightly. Let stand, uncovered, 35 minutes.

4. After 15 minutes, preheat oven to 350°F.

5. Use the palm of your hand or a spatula to gently flatten each cake into a circle. Poke a few holes in the surface with a fork. Bake 30 to 35 minutes, or until golden brown.

Preparation time: 15 minutes
(plus 35 minutes sitting time)
Baking time: 30 to 35 minutes
Makes about 12 johnny cakes

Cold Shrimp Salad/
Seviche de Camarones (Panama)

Panamanian diners enjoy this refreshing seafood salad as an appetizer or party dish. It is often served with buttered saltine crackers or in crispy tortilla shells.

1 lb. fresh shrimp, peeled and deveined,* or 1 lb. frozen cooked shrimp, thawed

juice of 3 lemons or 5 limes (½ to ⅔ c.)

1 white onion, minced

1 green pepper, seeded and finely chopped

1 tomato, finely chopped

1 avocado, peeled and chopped (optional)

1 chili pepper, minced (optional)

2 tbsp. fresh parsley, finely chopped

½ tsp. salt

¼ tsp. black pepper

1. If using frozen shrimp, skip to Step 2. If using fresh shrimp, bring a pot of water to a boil over high heat. Drop shrimp into boiling water and cook 5 to 7 minutes, or until pink. Drain and allow to cool slightly.

2. Chop shrimp into bite-sized pieces (or leave whole if they are small). Place in a large mixing bowl with all remaining ingredients and mix well. Make sure that all ingredients are well covered with juice, adding more if necessary.

3. Cover and refrigerate at least 4 hours. Serve chilled.

Preparation time: 20 to 30 minutes (plus 4 hours refrigeration time)
Serves 4 to 6

*If you use fresh shrimp for this recipe, you may be able to have it peeled and deveined at the grocery store. Otherwise, you can do it yourself. Hold the shrimp so that the underside is facing you. Starting at the head, use your fingers to peel off the shell from the head toward the tail. Then, using a sharp knife, carefully make a shallow cut all the way down the middle of the back. Hold the shrimp under cold running water to rinse out the dark vein.

Yucca Fritters/ *Carimañolas (Panama)*

Panamanian cooks often add their favorite seasonings—such as fresh cilantro or parsley, Worcestershire sauce, or chopped hard-boiled egg—to the carimañola filling.

2 to 2½ lb. yucca, peeled

2½ tsp. salt plus additional salt for filling

2 tbsp. corn oil

I onion, chopped

I clove garlic, minced

½ small green pepper, seeded and chopped (optional)

I lb. lean ground beef

I small tomato, chopped, or I tsp. tomato paste

I tsp. Tabasco or other hot sauce (optional)

¼ tsp. black pepper

corn or vegetable oil for frying

1. Cut yucca into chunks, removing any tough parts from the center of the yucca. Place chunks in a large pot with 1 tsp. of the salt and enough water to cover. Bring to a boil and boil 10 minutes longer. Add 1 c. cool water, return to a boil, and cook 5 minutes more. Add another cup cool water and boil another 5 minutes, or until yucca is very tender. (Adding the cool water helps soften the yucca.)

2. Remove from heat and drain in a colander. Transfer yucca to bowl and, using a potato masher or large fork, mash yucca to a soft paste. Sprinkle with 1 tsp. salt and knead until yucca has a doughy consistency. If it is too dry, add water 1 tsp. at a time. Wrap yucca in plastic wrap and refrigerate.

3. Heat oil over medium heat in a large, deep skillet. Add onion, garlic, and green pepper (if using). Sauté 3 to 4 minutes, or until soft but not brown. Add beef and use a spatula or wooden spoon to break meat apart. Cook 5 minutes, stirring occasionally. Add tomato or tomato paste, Tabasco (if desired), remaining salt (to taste), and black pepper. Mix all ingredients

well and cook 5 minutes longer, or until meat is well browned. Remove from heat.

4. Remove yucca dough from fridge and form into about 16 balls. Using your thumb, press a deep, round dent into the center of one ball. Place about 1 tbsp. of meat filling into the indentation and pinch the edges of the dough together to close. Gently roll the ball between your hands to shape it into an oval 3 to 4 inches long. Use a fork to poke a few holes in fritter (otherwise fritters may explode while cooking). Set aside. Repeat with remaining dough and filling.

5. Heat 2 to 3 tbsp. of oil in a skillet over medium heat. Place as many fritters in the pan as will fit comfortably and cook 2 to 3 minutes on each side, or until crispy and golden brown.* Remove from pan and place on paper towels to drain. If extra oil is necessary to cook all the fritters, let the pan cool before adding more. Serve hot.

*For reduced-fat carimañolas, try baking them instead of frying. Preheat oven to 400°F. Roll fritters gently in a little flour, dip briefly into lightly beaten egg whites, and then roll gently in a little dish of bread crumbs. Place on a lightly greased baking sheet and coat fritters lightly with nonfat cooking spray. Bake 20 minutes, or until golden.

Preparation time: 45 minutes to 1 hour
Cooking time: 1¼ to 1½ hours
Serves 6

Fried Plantains/*Plátanos Fritos* (Guatemala)

Crispy fried plantains are popular throughout Central America. This very simple recipe is typically Guatemalan, but cooks in neighboring countries often add their own twists to this basic version. Some prefer unripe green plantains to ripe, while others fry the plantains twice.

2 ripe (yellow-and-black skinned)
    plantains

3 tbsp. corn oil

1. Peel plantains and cut diagonally into ½-inch thick slices.*

2. Place oil in skillet over medium heat. Add plantains and sauté for 3 to 4 minutes on each side, or until golden brown. Remove from pan and place on paper towels to drain. Serve hot and sprinkle with salt if desired.**

Preparation time: 5 to 10 minutes
Cooking time: 6 to 8 minutes
Serves 4

*The best way to peel plantains varies depending on how they are being used. For this dish, use a sharp knife to slit the peel lengthwise, from one end of the plantain to the other. Next, slice the plantain diagonally into ovals and use your fingers to peel each piece.

**Fried plantains are also eaten as a sweet treat in Guatemala. To make plantains for dessert, omit the salt. Instead, after cooking spread a thin layer of sour cream over plantains and sprinkle with sugar.

Stuffed Tortillas and Slaw / Pupusas con Salsa y Curtido de Repollo (El Salvador)

This Salvadoran specialty is found throughout the nation, where diners enjoy spicing up their pupusas with plenty of hot sauce and then cooling down with a bite of refreshing curtido (slaw). Cheese is the simplest and most common filling, but local cooks also prepare pupusas with black or refried beans, potatoes, fried pork, or a mixture of fillings.

Curtido:

½ head green cabbage, shredded

2 carrots, grated

I white onion or 3 green onions, sliced thinly

I c. cider vinegar or white vinegar

½ c. water

I tsp. salt

I tsp. oregano

I tsp. crushed red pepper flakes

Pupusas:

4 c. masa harina (finely ground cornmeal)

½ tsp. salt

2½ c. warm water

1½ c. grated soft white cheese, such as Monterey Jack or mozzarella

2 tbsp. corn or vegetable oil

Tabasco, or other hot sauce

1. To make curtido, combine all ingredients in a large bowl and mix well. Cover and refrigerate for at least 6 hours.

2. To prepare pupusas, combine masa, salt, and water in a large mixing bowl. Knead mixture (still in bowl or on a clean countertop) for 2 to 4 minutes, or until a smooth, soft dough forms. If the dough is too hard or dry, add 1 tbsp. of water at a time until dough is moist but not too runny. If dough is too runny, add 1 tbsp. masa at a time. Cover with a clean dish towel and allow to sit for 10 to 15 minutes.

3. Form dough into balls that are the size of an egg. Holding a ball in one hand, use your other thumb to press a dent into the center of the dough. Keep making the indentation deeper and wider, until the dough is in the shape of a small cup. Fill the "cup" with 1 to 2 tsp. cheese and close it by pressing the edges of the dough firmly together.

Gently roll the ball between your hands and flatten it by patting both sides, until the dough is about 3 to 4 inches in diameter and ¼- to ½-inch thick. Make sure to flatten the pupusas, or they will not cook all the way through. Repeat with remaining dough and filling.*

4. Heat oil in a large skillet over medium heat. Place one or two pupusas in the skillet and sauté 2 to 3 minutes on each side, or until golden brown. Drain on paper towels. Repeat with remaining pupusas, adding more oil to the pan if necessary. Serve hot with hot sauce and curtido on the side.

*Preparation time: 1 hour
(plus 6 hours refrigeration time)
Cooking time: 45 minutes to 1 hour
Serves 6*

If you are having trouble filling the pupusas this way, you may want to try a different method. Divide each ball of dough in half and flatten both pieces into rounds 3 to 4 inches in diameter and ¼-inch thick. Place 1 to 2 tsp. filling in the center of one round. Cover with the other round, and press the edges together to seal firmly. It may also help to moisten your fingers with a little bit of water as you seal the edges.

Main Dishes

Central American entrées are rich in variety. Most of the region's cooking is based on a few standard ingredients, the most basic of which are tortillas, beans, and rice. Throughout Central America, cooks use these staples to create fresh, fantastic meals. Beans appear in dishes such as the standard bean soup, which shows up on menus around the region. Rice and beans appear together in *gallo pinto*, whose name—which literally means "painted rooster"—may have come from its speckled light-and-dark appearance. And in most of the region's countries, tortillas are a part of every meal.

Beyond this basic foundation, many Central American entrées highlight meat or seafood, from Guatemalan *hilachas*, which drenches thin strips of beef in a flavorful tomato sauce, to crispy Belizean fried fish. However, many regional main dishes can also easily be prepared without meat. Popular Honduran enchiladas, for example, are often topped with chicken or beef but are just as tasty in a vegetarian version using—for example—rice and beans.

This hearty chicken stew from Guatemala can also be made as a vegetarian dish. (Recipe on page 48.)

Grilled Beef with Parsley Sauce/
Churrasco con Chimichurri (Nicaragua)

This traditional grilled entrée is a Nicaraguan classic. Variations on the dish are also prepared throughout the region.

1 small white onion, minced

2 cloves garlic, peeled and mashed

½ c. fresh parsley, minced

¼ c. vegetable or olive oil

6 tbsp. red wine vinegar

1 tsp. salt plus additional salt for steak

½ tsp. black pepper plus additional pepper for steak

1 lb. beef tenderloin

1. In a large mixing bowl, combine onion, garlic, parsley, oil, vinegar, salt, and black pepper. Mix thoroughly, cover, and refrigerate for at least 6 hours.

2. Have an experienced cook start a charcoal or gas grill, if using.

3. Trim all visible fat from tenderloin and cut into four thin steaks, each no more than ½-inch thick. Gently pat each steak with some salt and pepper.

4. Set the oven to broil, if using.

5. Have an adult help you place steaks directly on a grill, or, if broiling, on a baking sheet or broiler pan. Cook 4 to 6 minutes on each side, or until cooked through. Watch carefully to avoid burning. Serve hot, with chimichurri (parsley sauce) on the side.

*Chimichurri has many variations. To experiment with the flavor of yours, try adding the juice of 1 small lime or lemon, 1 minced chili pepper, 1 tsp. red pepper flakes, 1 chopped tomato, 2 bay leaves, or 1 tsp. dried oregano to the basic parsley mixture.

Preparation time: 15 minutes
(plus 6 hours refrigeration)
Cooking time: 15 to 20 minutes
Serves 4

minutes or until thick. If sauce is still too runny, add 2 tsp. of flour at a time until thickened. Remove from heat.

6. Drain the chicken, reserving the stock. Return chicken to stockpot.

7. Add 1 c. of stock to vegetable puree. Add cinnamon, salt, and black pepper and mix well. Transfer this sauce to the stockpot, covering chicken well. Cover stockpot, place over medium heat, and simmer gently for 20 minutes, or until chicken is tender. Add a little more stock if mixture gets too dry.

8. Meanwhile, in separate pot, boil potatoes and zucchini 10 minutes. Add green beans and boil another 10 minutes, or until all ingredients are tender. Drain cooked vegetables, add to chicken and sauce and mix well. Transfer all to a large serving dish and serve with white rice.

Preparation time: 45 to 55 minutes
Cooking time: 1½ hours
Serves 6

*After handling raw chicken or other poultry, always remember to wash your hands, utensils, and preparation area thoroughly with soapy hot water. Also, when checking chicken for doneness, it's a good idea to cut it open to make sure that the meat is white (not pink) all the way through.

**Look for pumpkin seeds, called pepitas in Spanish, in your grocery store or in Latin American or Mexican markets.

***To peel a tomato, carefully cut X-shaped slits on the top and bottom of the tomato. Using a slotted spoon, lower the tomato into boiling water and allow to sit for up to 30 seconds. Remove. When the tomato is cool enough to handle, you should be able to peel off the skin with your fingers.

Fried Fish / *Pescado Frito* (Belize)

With miles of coastline, Central America is a great place for seafood lovers. Belizean cooks prepare this simple fried fish with the freshest catches of the day.

4 to 6 fish fillets (about 1 lb.)*

2 c. flour or 2 c. unseasoned bread crumbs

1 tbsp. salt

2 tsp. black pepper

4 limes (2 for juice, 2 cut into wedges)

2 large eggs

6 tbsp. milk

corn or vegetable oil for frying**

1. Wash fish under cool running water and pat dry with paper towels.

2. In a dish that is wide enough to dip fish fillets into, mix together flour or bread crumbs, salt, and black pepper. Add juice of 2 limes and mix well.

3. In a small bowl, beat eggs with a fork or whisk. Add milk and stir well. Transfer egg mixture to a second dish wide enough for the fillets.

4. Roll each fillet in the flour or bread crumb mixture. Next, dip into egg mixture, covering both sides. Return to flour mixture and press firmly to coat well.

5. Pour oil about ¼ inch deep in a large skillet and heat over high heat. Carefully add one or two fillets to hot oil and fry 3 minutes on each side, or until golden. Repeat with remaining fillets. Drain on paper towels and serve hot with lime wedges and johnny cakes (see page 33).

Any whitefish, such as tilapia, cod, sole, snapper, or flounder, will work for this recipe.

**Cooking with hot oil is simple and safe as long as you're careful. Always have an adult help you. Be sure to use long-handled utensils whenever possible. Stand back from the stove as far as you can and try to place fish into oil slowly to avoid splattering.*

Preparation time: 15 to 20 minutes
Cooking time: 20 to 25 minutes
Serves 4 to 6

Shredded Beef in Tomato Sauce/Hilachas (Guatemala)

Hilachas is a favorite Guatemalan dish, rich with tomato, garlic, and the fresh taste of cilantro.

2 lb. beef (any cut, such as chuck, round, or flank steak), sliced into several large pieces

6 medium tomatoes, peeled and roughly chopped

1 onion, sliced thin

3 cloves garlic, sliced thin

½ tsp. salt plus additional salt for seasoning

8 c. water

2 tbsp. oil

½ lb. tomatillos, husked

1 chili, seeded and sliced thinly*

3 to 4 tbsp. cilantro, finely chopped

2 lb. potatoes

black pepper

*Choose chiles of whatever spiciness you prefer. Also, be careful when working with chiles. The oil in the seeds and fibers is what makes them spicy, and it can also irritate your skin and eyes. Wear rubber gloves while cutting the peppers, and be sure to wash your hands well when you are done.

1. In a large stockpot, combine beef, two tomatoes, onion, garlic, salt, and water. Cover and bring to a boil over high heat. Reduce heat and simmer 35 minutes.

2. Remove beef from pot. When meat is cool enough to handle, tear into thin, bite-sized strips.

3. Heat oil over medium heat in a large skillet. Add remaining tomatoes, tomatillos, chili, and cilantro. Sauté 5 to 7 minutes. Transfer to a food processor and process to a smooth, liquid sauce.

4. Place unpeeled potatoes in another large stockpot with enough water to cover. Bring to a boil and cook 15 to 20 minutes, or until tender. Remove from pot and run under cool water. When cool enough to handle, peel and cube potatoes.

5. Combine potatoes, tomato sauce, and beef with the mixture in the first stockpot. Season with salt and black pepper to taste. Bring to a boil, simmer 8 to 10 more minutes, and serve hot with white rice.

Preparation time: 30 minutes
Cooking time: 1 hour
Serves 6

Bean Soup / *Sopa de Frijoles*

Variations on this basic soup are found in every Central American country. For example, Nicaraguans prefer red beans to black and sometimes add pork or beef, while Costa Rican cooks are especially fond of fresh cilantro.

2 tbsp. corn oil

1 red or green bell pepper, seeded and chopped

1 small yellow onion, chopped

3 or 4 cloves garlic, minced

3 15-oz. cans black or red beans, drained

7 c. water

4 green onions, chopped

½ c. fresh cilantro, chopped

2 tsp. salt

1 tsp. black pepper

4 to 6 large eggs (optional)

1. In a large saucepan or stockpot, heat oil over medium heat. Add bell pepper, onion, and garlic. Sauté 3 to 4 minutes.

2. Add beans and water to pot and stir well. Raise heat to high and bring to a boil. Reduce heat, cover, and simmer 30 minutes.

3. Add about half of the green onions, half the cilantro, and salt and pepper. Stir well, cover, and simmer 5 minutes more.

4. If using eggs, crack 1 egg per person into the pot. Try to place each egg in a separate part of the pot. Cover and cook, without stirring, 2 or 3 minutes longer, or until egg yolks are cooked through. To serve, ladle soup and one egg into each diner's bowl. Garnish with remaining green onions and cilantro.

Preparation time: 20 minutes
Cooking time: 45 minutes
Serves 4 to 6

Desserts and Drinks

In a region of plentiful sugarcane plantations, it's hardly surprising that most Central American diners have quite a sweet tooth. To satisfy that craving, local cooks prepare a tempting array of desserts. Spanish settlers also brought a taste for butter, eggs, and cream. These rich ingredients feature highly in sweets such as tres leches, a cake drenched in three kinds of milk and topped with a sugary frosting. Desserts made with easy-to-find ingredients, such as baked bananas, rice pudding, and sweet potato *pone* (a puddinglike dish), are also favorites.

The steamy Central American climate has also resulted in a wide variety of refreshing drinks. Cool, cinnamon-flavored rice milk, called horchata, is drunk throughout the region. *Pinolillo*, on the other hand, is a Nicaraguan specialty made from the regional staples of cornmeal and cocoa. On cool winter nights, hot chocolate is a welcome treat. Often flavored with vanilla, cinnamon, and dried chili peppers, this sweet and spicy beverage has been made in Central America since the days of the ancient Maya. Other popular beverages include fresh-squeezed juice from tropical fruits such as pineapple, guava, mango, or papaya.

Three milks cake is a favorite dessert throughout Central America. (Recipe on page 56.)

Three Milks Cake/Pastel de Tres Leches (Nicaragua and Costa Rica)

This rich dessert is considered a specialty in Nicaragua and Costa Rica, but it is found throughout Central America.

Cake:

1 c. flour

1 tsp. baking powder

5 large eggs, separated*

1 c. sugar

½ c. milk

1 tsp. vanilla extract

Milk Syrup:**

1 12-oz. can evaporated milk

1 14-oz. can sweetened condensed milk

1 c. heavy cream or whole milk

Frosting:

1 c. cold whipping or heavy cream

¼ c. sugar

½ tsp. vanilla extract (optional)

1. Preheat oven to 350°F and lightly grease a 9-inch square cake pan.

2. In a medium bowl, sift together flour and baking powder.

3. In a large mixing bowl, use an electric mixer on medium speed to beat egg whites until fluffy and forming soft peaks. Add sugar 1 tbsp. at a time and beat until mixed well. Add egg yolks one at a time, beating 30 seconds after each addition. Still beating, add half of the flour mixture and half of the milk to the eggs. Mix well. Add remaining flour mixture, remaining milk, and vanilla extract, and mix well.

4. Pour cake batter into prepared pan and bake 20 to 25 minutes, or until a toothpick inserted into the center of the cake comes out clean. Remove from oven and allow to cool on wire rack. Use a fork or a toothpick to poke a few holes in the cake's surface.

5. In a large mixing bowl, combine evaporated milk, sweetened condensed milk, and cream or milk.

Blend well with a wire whisk and slowly pour over cake. Cover and refrigerate for at least 2 hours. (Because of all the milk in this cake, it is very important to keep it refrigerated.)

6. Shortly before serving cake, place whipping cream, sugar, and vanilla (if using) in a chilled medium mixing bowl. Use an electric mixer to whip until peaks just begin to stiffen. (Do not overbeat, or cream will curdle.) Use a rubber spatula or a knife to spread frosting over cake surface. Cut into squares and serve. Store any leftover cake in the refrigerator.

Preparation time: 35 to 40 minutes
(plus 2 hours refrigeration)
Baking time: 20 to 25 minutes
Serves 9

*To separate an egg, crack it cleanly on the edge of a nonplastic bowl. Holding the two halves of the eggshell over the bowl, gently pour the egg yolk back and forth between the two halves, letting the egg white drip into the bowl and being careful not to break the yolk. When most of the egg white has been separated, drop yolk into a second bowl.

**The three milks that make up tres leches are tasty but high in fat and calories. To lighten the dish, use skim or reduced-fat varieties of all three. You can also cut back the fat by serving each piece of cake with a small dollop of prepared, reduced-fat whipped topping instead of frosting the entire cake.

Baked Bananas / Bananas al Horno

Living in one of the world's biggest banana-producing areas, Central American cooks have created many delicious banana dishes. This is one of the simplest and most delightful.*

2 ripe bananas

1 tbsp. cold butter plus extra for pan

2 tbsp. sugar (white or brown)

1 tsp. ground cinnamon

1 tbsp. milk

1. Preheat oven to 350°F. Lightly grease a square glass baking dish with butter.

2. Slice bananas in half the long way. Place them, cut side down, in the baking dish.

3. Spread each banana half with a little butter. Sprinkle with sugar and cinnamon, and drizzle milk over all. Bake 10 to 15 minutes, or until golden brown.

Preparation time: 10 minutes
Baking time: 10 to 15 minutes
Serves 4

*It's easy to add your own touch to this recipe. Some cooks substitute the milk, sugar, and cinnamon with 1 tsp. lemon juice and 1 tbsp. honey. Others serve the dish with garnishes of nuts and raisins. Try these or other variations to find your favorites.

Rice Milk/Horchata (El Salvador)

Although rice milk is especially popular in El Salvador, it is also common in neighboring countries. This refreshing beverage is perfect for cooling your tongue after a spicy dish.

1 c. uncooked rice

1 cinnamon stick or 2 tsp. ground cinnamon

5 c. water

½ c. sugar (approximately)

1 tsp. vanilla extract

1. Place rice and cinnamon in a blender. Process until ground to a fine powder.

2. Transfer rice powder to a large bowl or saucepan. Add water and mix well. Cover and refrigerate at least 4 hours.

3. Place rice mixture in a blender and process for a few seconds, or until well blended.

4. Place a piece of cheesecloth or a coffee filter over a large bowl or pitcher. Carefully pour rice mixture through the cloth or filter to strain. (If this step is skipped, the milk will have a chalky texture.)

5. Discard strained rice and cinnamon and return liquid to blender. Add sugar to taste and vanilla extract and process a few seconds more. Filter a second time and discard cloth or filter. Serve in tall ice-filled glasses.

Preparation time: 20 minutes
(plus 4 hours refrigeration time)
Serves 4

*For a simple variation, add ½ tsp. almond extract with the sugar and vanilla. Some Central American cooks also like to garnish horchata with toasted pumpkin seeds.

Corn and Cocoa Drink / Pinolillo (Nicaragua)

This unusual beverage is found throughout Nicaragua. While many locals take their pinolillo without sugar, you'll probably want to sweeten yours at first. Some people also like to add a dash of ground cloves to the mix.

1 c. masa harina, or fine white
    cornmeal

½ c. unsweetened cocoa powder

1 c. sugar

¼ tsp. ground cinnamon

6 c. milk*

1. Place masa in a large skillet over medium heat and cook, stirring constantly, for 3 to 5 minutes, or until lightly toasted. Remove from heat.

2. Place toasted masa in a blender. Add remaining ingredients and blend until frothy. (If you don't have a blender, you can combine ingredients in a large pitcher and mix well.)

3. Chill pinolillo for at least 1 hour. Stir well before serving.

Preparation time: 10 minutes
(plus 1 hour chilling time)
Serves 4 to 6

To reduce the fat content, use skim milk in your pinolillo. For a dairy-free drink, you can also use soy milk, rice milk, or water.

Holiday and Festival Food

With special occasions ranging from ancient Mayan festivals to Catholic feasts, Central Americans have plenty of reason to celebrate. Fortunately for the hungry festivalgoer, each event is filled with tasty treats. Some are as simple as polvorones, sweet little cookies that don't take long to make. Others, such as tamales, require more work and more time, but they yield delicious results.

Even the harder dishes are worth preparing, both for their delicious flavor and for their long history and important role in local tradition. Try making these Central American classics for a special event or anytime. Once you've gotten familiar with the recipes, perhaps they'll become part of your own tradition.

These cornmeal packets are filled with meat and vegetables. (Recipe on page 66.)

Mayan Chicken Soup/*Caldo Kash* (Guatemala)

This Mayan recipe is hundreds of years old, and the soup is so tasty that it's not hard to see why Guatemalan cooks are still making it. This dish—which is traditionally made very spicy—is served for a wide range of Mayan and other special occasions.

1 lb. boneless, skinless chicken breasts, cut into large chunks

8 c. water or chicken stock

2 cloves garlic, finely chopped

½ tsp. achiote paste*

1 tsp. salt

1 large yellow onion, sliced

⅓ c. fresh oregano, chopped, or 2 tbsp. dried oregano

⅓ c. fresh basil, chopped, or 2 tbsp. dried basil

⅓ c. fresh chives, chopped

1 small dried chili pepper, minced, or 1 to 2 tsp. crushed red pepper flakes (optional)

½ tsp. black pepper

1. Place chicken and water or stock in a large stockpot. Bring to a boil over high heat, add garlic, and boil uncovered for 10 minutes.

2. Add achiote paste and salt. Mix well and boil 10 minutes longer. Add onion, oregano, basil, chives, chili pepper (if using), and black pepper. Reduce heat to medium and cook 15 or 20 minutes longer, or until chicken is cooked all the way through. Season with more salt and pepper if necessary, and serve hot with corn tortillas.

Preparation time: 20 minutes
Cooking time: 45 to 55 minutes
Serves 4

*Achiote paste (also called annatto paste) is a Mayan staple, made from achiote seeds mixed with other spices. Look for it in the international cooking section of your grocery store or in Mexican and Latin American markets. If you can't find it, you can substitute 1 tsp. of ground annatto seed, which is available in the spice section of most grocery stores.

Rice and Chicken/Arroz con Pollo (Panama)

This dish, one of Panama's most popular traditional entrées, is served on nearly all special occasions, from Christmas to family birthday celebrations.

3 tbsp. olive oil

1½ lb. boneless, skinless chicken breasts

1 red or green bell pepper, seeded and chopped

1 yellow onion, chopped

3 or 4 cloves garlic, minced

3 fresh tomatoes, diced, or 15 oz. canned diced tomatoes

8 oz. canned tomato sauce

⅛ tsp. saffron or ¾ tsp. turmeric

1 bay leaf

1 tsp. salt

½ tsp. black pepper

2 c. uncooked rice

4 c. chicken broth or water

1 c. frozen green peas, thawed

½ c. green olives with pimentos, sliced

2 tbsp. capers

3 tbsp. fresh cilantro, chopped (optional)

1. In a stockpot or large, deep skillet, heat oil over medium heat. Add chicken and sauté 7 to 10 minutes, or until lightly browned. Turn regularly to cook evenly.

2. Add bell pepper, onion, and garlic. Sauté 3 to 4 minutes longer, or until onions and peppers are soft but not brown. Add tomatoes, tomato sauce, saffron, bay leaf, salt, and pepper, and stir well. Cook 2 to 3 minutes, stirring often.

3. Add rice and broth or water to pot. Mix well, raise heat to high, and bring to a boil. Reduce heat until mixture is simmering, cover, and cook 10 minutes. Stir in peas, olives, capers, and cilantro (if using) and cook 10 more minutes, or until rice is tender and chicken is done (not pink in the middle). If you like, you can remove chicken and tear into chunks before returning it to pot. Serve hot, with extra olives, capers, and cilantro, if desired.

Preparation time: 10 minutes
Cooking time: 35 to 45 minutes
Serves 4 to 6

Cornmeal Packets / Tamales (Panama)

These delicious treats are a traditional Christmas meal in households throughout Central America and are also enjoyed by many families for the Day of the Dead. Like many regional recipes, there are seemingly endless variations, but this version is typically Panamanian. Local cooks wrap tamales in banana or plantain leaves, but beginners will find aluminum foil much easier.

Dough:

2 c. masa harina

1 tsp. salt

½ c. (1 stick) butter or vegetable shortening, melted

1 c. chicken stock or water, warmed

Filling:

3 tbsp. corn oil

1 lb. lean pork loin, cut into 1-inch pieces*

2 cloves garlic, minced

1 onion, chopped

1 small red bell pepper, seeded and chopped

1 small green bell pepper, seeded and chopped

2 c. water

1 tomato, chopped

1 small jalapeño or other chili pepper, minced (optional)

1. In a large mixing bowl, combine masa, salt, and butter. Use an electric mixer to beat well. Add stock or water gradually until you have a smooth, firm dough. Cover and set aside.

2. Heat oil in a deep saucepan or stockpot over medium heat. Add pork and sauté 12 to 15 minutes, or until lightly browned. Add garlic, onion, and bell peppers to pot. Sauté 3 to 4 minutes, or until onions are beginning to soften.

3. Add water, tomato, chili pepper (if using), cilantro, salt, and black pepper to pot. Stir well, reduce heat to medium-low, and cover. Simmer 30 minutes, or until meat is tender and cooked all the way through and sauce has thickened.

4. Remove pork from heat and drain, reserving about ½ c. of sauce. Add this reserved sauce to the masa dough. Knead dough (in bowl or on a clean countertop) until it is moist and a little bit soft, but not runny.

1 tbsp. fresh cilantro, finely chopped

1 tsp. salt

¼ tsp. black pepper

3 tbsp. green olives with pimentos
(about 12 olives)

2 tbsp. raisins

Other:

6 pieces of aluminum foil about 12-
by 12-inches square each

*For vegetarian tamales, try using
filling such as tofu, mock duck, cooked
black beans and rice, cheese, or
vegetables in place of the pork.

5. Lay one piece of foil on a clean
work surface. Place a large spoonful
of masa dough in the center of the
sheet. Flatten and shape the dough
to a rough 6- by 4-inch rectangle.
Place 2 heaping tbsp. of meat and
vegetables on the dough. Garnish
with 2 or 3 olives and a few raisins.
Place another spoonful of dough on
top and press the edges together
lightly to enclose filling. Fold the
right and left sides of the foil firmly
over the tamale. Fold up the two
open ends to cover the seam on top
tightly. Repeat with remaining
dough and filling. You should have
enough dough to make about six
tamales.

6. Bring a large pot of water to boil.
Gently place the tamales in the
water and boil for 40 minutes. Use
tongs to remove tamales from water
and set aside until cool enough to
handle. Unwrap and eat warm.

Preparation time: 1¼ to 1½ hours
Cooking time: 1 hour
Serves 6

Powdered Sugar Cookies / *Polvorones*

These sugar-covered cookies—whose name comes from polvo, the Spanish word for "dust," are indeed a bit messy. But they're worth it! Many Central Americans enjoy polvorones during Semana Santa and at Easter.

1 c. (2 sticks) butter or margarine, at room temperature

1½ c. powdered sugar, plus extra for rolling

1 tsp. vanilla extract

2 c. flour

¼ tsp. salt

1. Preheat oven to 350°F.

2. In a large mixing bowl, combine butter, sugar, and vanilla. Use an electric mixer to beat until light and fluffy.

3. Gradually stir in flour and salt until you have a firm, stiff dough. If the dough is too runny or soft to hold its shape, add 1 tsp. of flour at a time until firm.

4. Roll dough between your palms to shape into walnut-sized balls. Place on ungreased baking sheets and bake 15 to 20 minutes, or until bottoms are lightly browned.

5. Place extra powdered sugar in a bowl or a wide, shallow dish.

6. Remove cookies from oven and allow to cool for 2 or 3 minutes. When cookies are cool enough to handle but still warm, roll them in the powdered sugar until completely covered. Cool on wire racks and serve.

*Some cooks add ingredients such as ½ c. ground almonds, ½ tsp. ground cinnamon, or 1 tbsp. grated lemon or orange zest to the dough in Step 3. Try these variations for a different twist on polvorones.

Preparation time: 30 minutes
Baking time: 15 to 20 minutes
Makes 3 to 4 dozen

Index

About the Authors

Alison Behnke is an author and editor of children's books. She also enjoys traveling and experiencing new cultures and cuisines. Her other cookbooks include *Cooking the Cuban Way*, *Cooking the Brazilian Way*, and *Vegetarian Cooking around the World*. She has also written geography books, including *Italy in Pictures* and *Afghanistan in Pictures*.

Griselda Aracely Chacon lives in the beautiful colonial city of Antigua, Guatemala. She is employed as an administrative assistant at Obras Sociales del Hermano Pedro, a charitable institution serving the poor and disabled of Guatemala. Chacon is a mother of six, and on her days off, she enjoys cooking with her husband, using the freshest of ingredients found in the many local outdoor markets.

Kristina Anderson has been a missionary in Guatemala for the past three years. She has worked as a medical interpreter in the charitable institution Obras Sociales del Hermano Pedro and as a special education teacher for people with disabilities who live in the institution. Anderson enjoys local Guatemalan cuisine.

Photo Acknowledgments

The photographs in this book are reproduced with the permission of: © Richard Bickel/CORBIS, p. 2–3; © Walter, Louiseann Pietrowicz/September 8th Stock, pp. 4 (both), 5 (both), 6, 18, 30, 35, 38, 42, 47, 50, 54, 59, 62, and 68; © Kruel Collection/Independent Picture Service, p. 9; © Bettmann/CORBIS, p. 10; © Reuters/CORBIS, p. 12; © Jeremy Horner/CORBIS, p. 15; © Arvind Garg/CORBIS, p. 26.

Cover photos (front, back, spine): © Walter, Louiseann Pietrowicz/ September 8th Stock.

The illustrations on pages 7, 19, 27, 31, 32, 34, 37, 39, 41, 43, 44, 45, 46, 49, 51, 51, 55, 57, 58, 60, 61, 63, 64, 67, and 69 are by Tim Seeley. The map on page 8 is by Bill Hauser.